Be An outlier

Erwin

OUTLIER

OUTLIER

FROM THE BEGINNING

Eddie Winkley

gatekeeper press™

Columbus, Ohio

This book is a work of fiction. The names, characters and events in this book are the products of the author's imagination or are used fictitiously. Any similarity to real persons living or dead is coincidental and not intended by the author.

Outlier: From the Beginning

Published by Gatekeeper Press
2167 Stringtown Rd, Suite 109
Columbus, OH 43123-2989
www.GatekeeperPress.com

The editorial work for this book is entirely the product of the author. Gatekeeper Press did not participate in and is not responsible for any aspect of this element.

ISBN (hardcover): 9781662917257

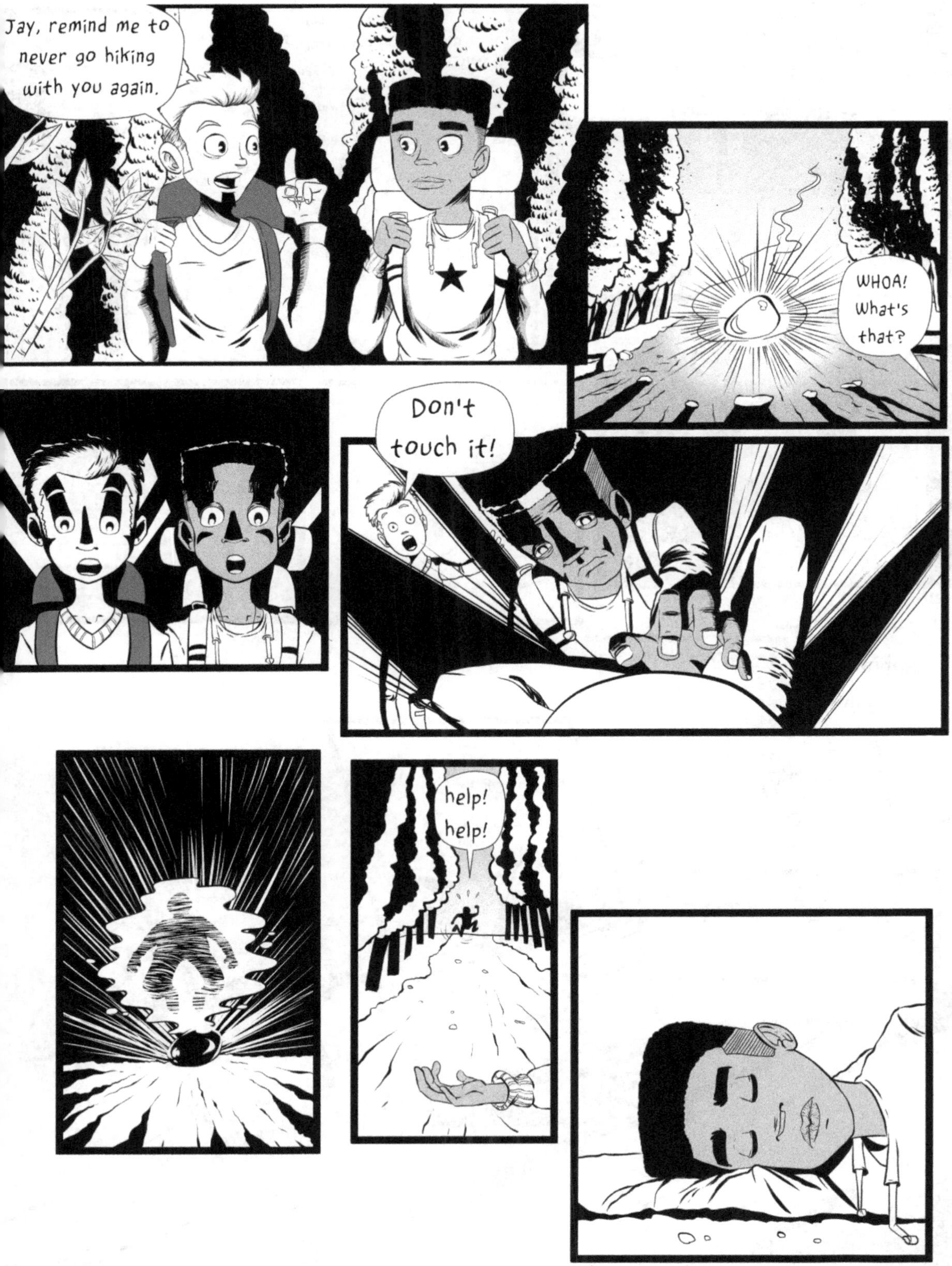
Jay, remind me to never go hiking with you again.
WHOA! What's that?
Don't touch it!
help! help!

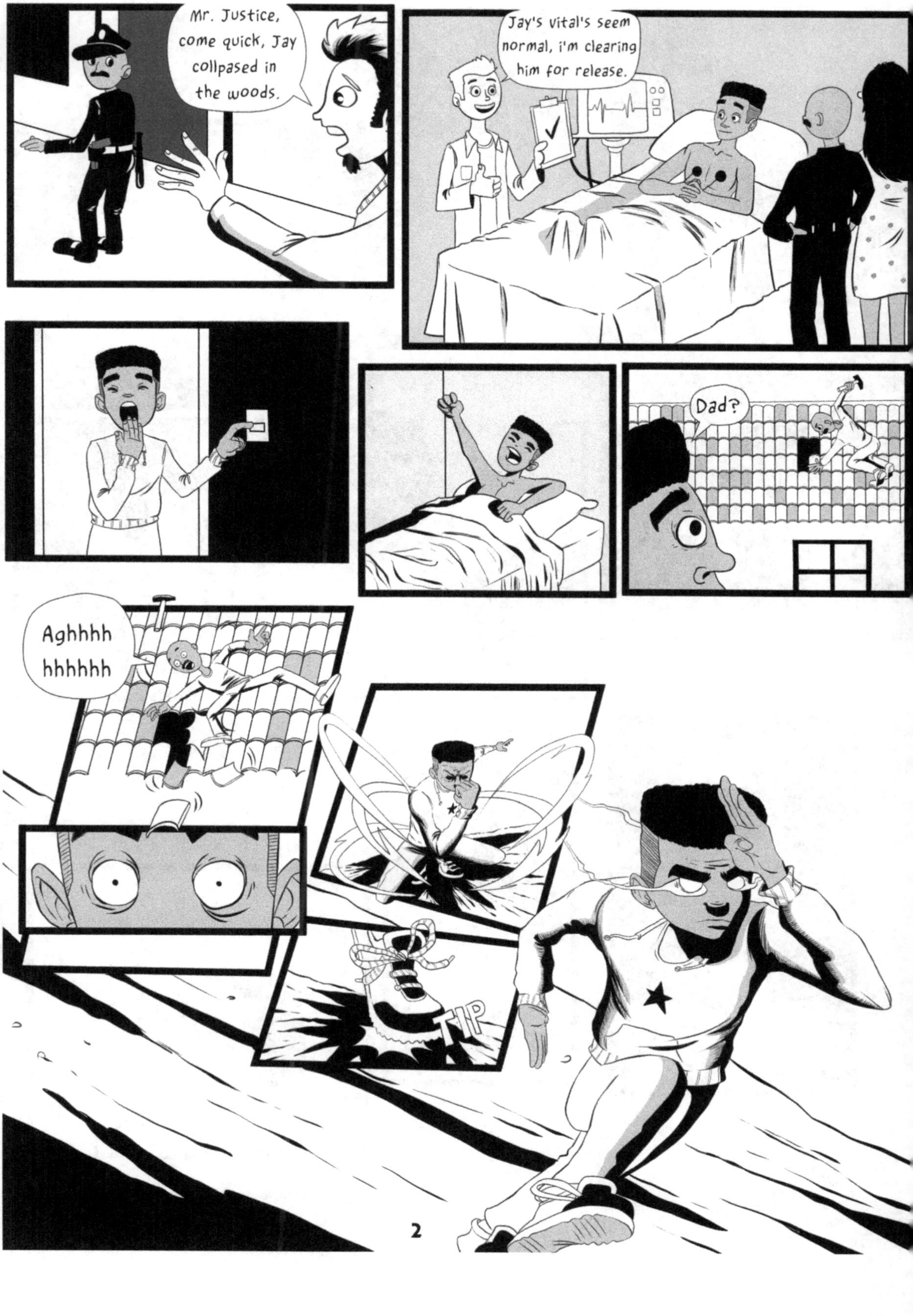
Mr. Justice, come quick, Jay collpased in the woods.
Jay's vital's seem normal, i'm clearing him for release.
Dad?
Aghhhh hhhhhh
TIP

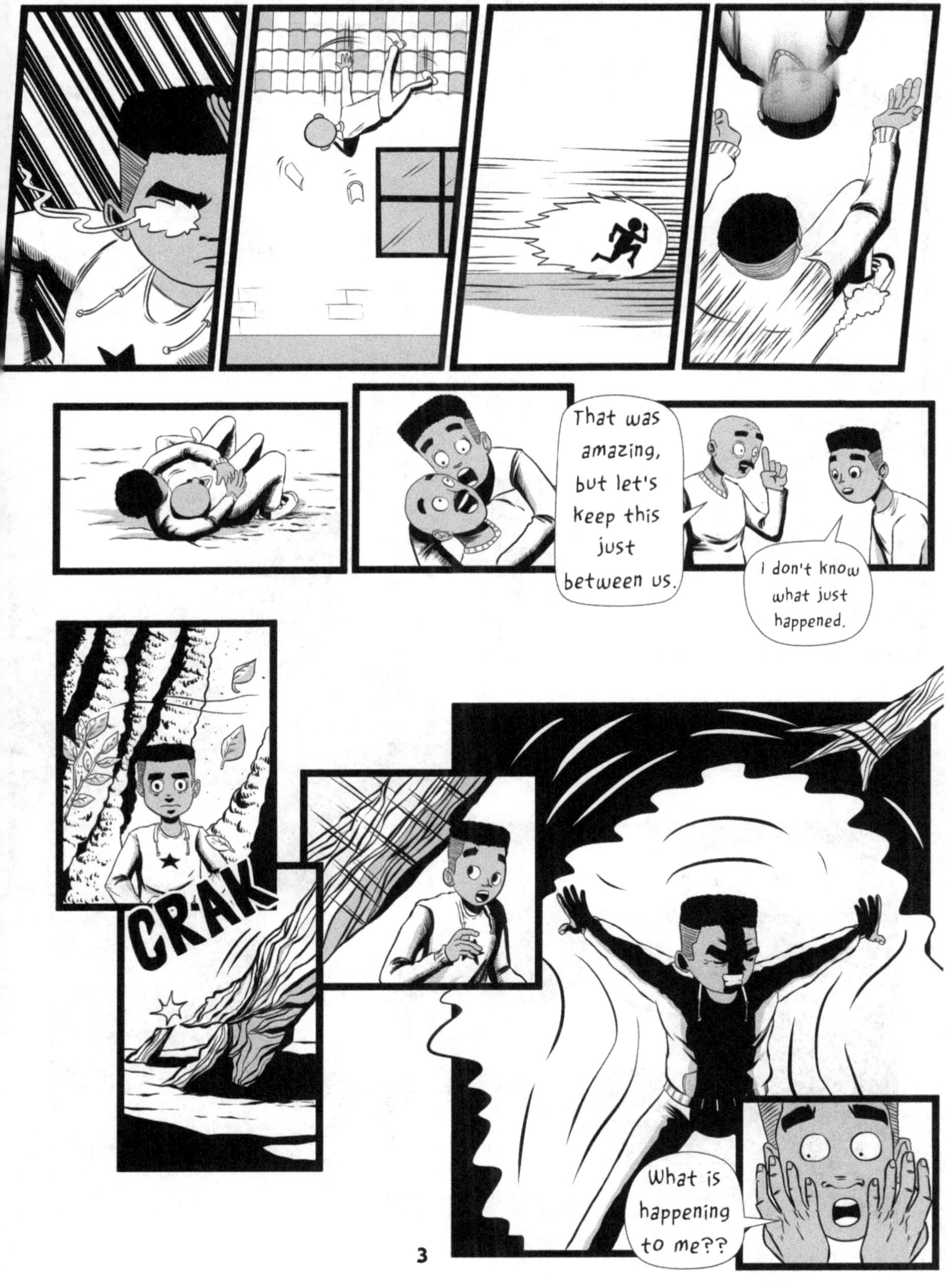

That was amazing, but let's keep this just between us.
I don't know what just happened.
CRAK
What is happening to me??

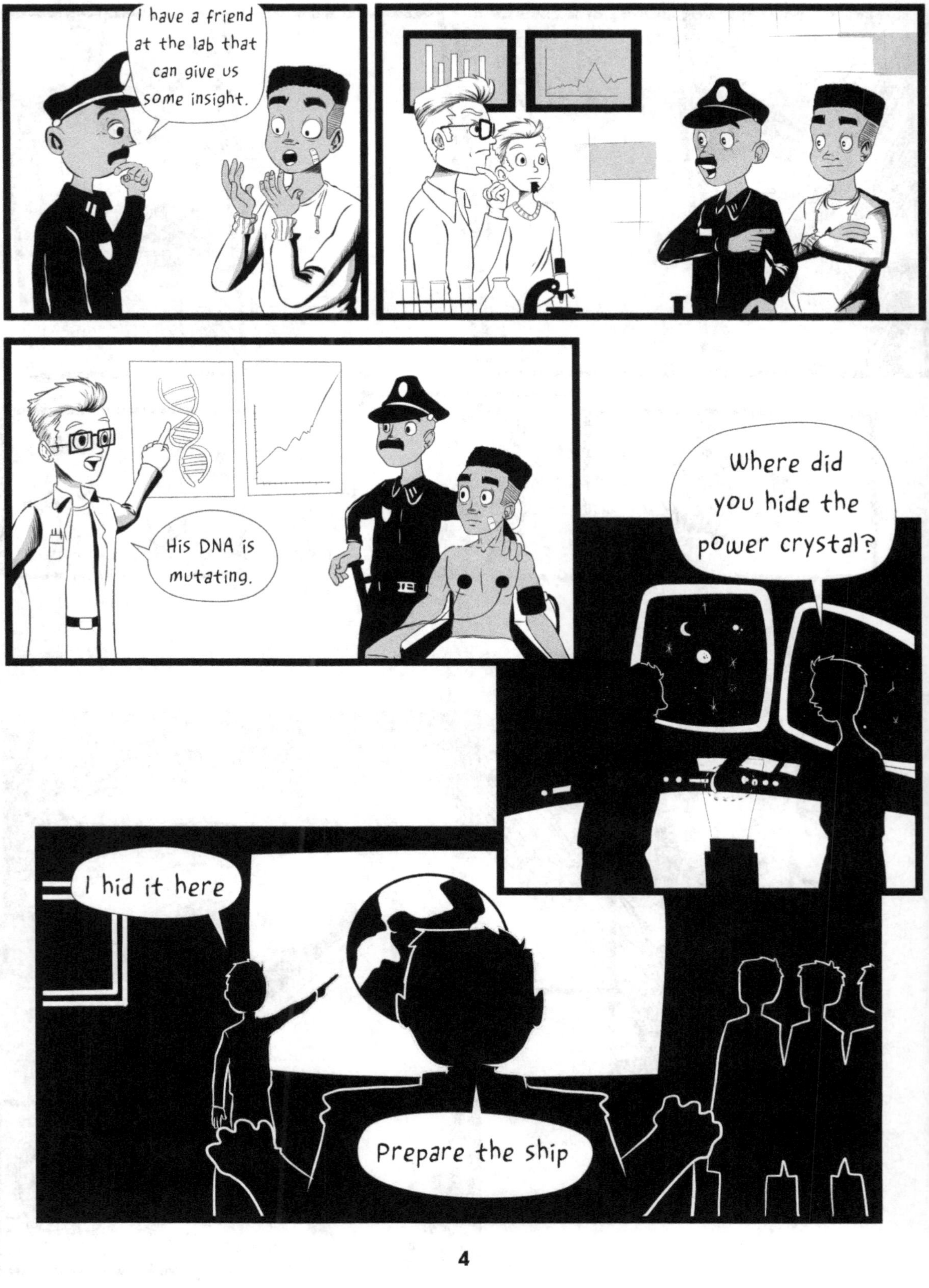
I have a friend at the lab that can give us some insight.
His DNA is mutating.
Where did you hide the power crystal?
I hid it here
Prepare the ship

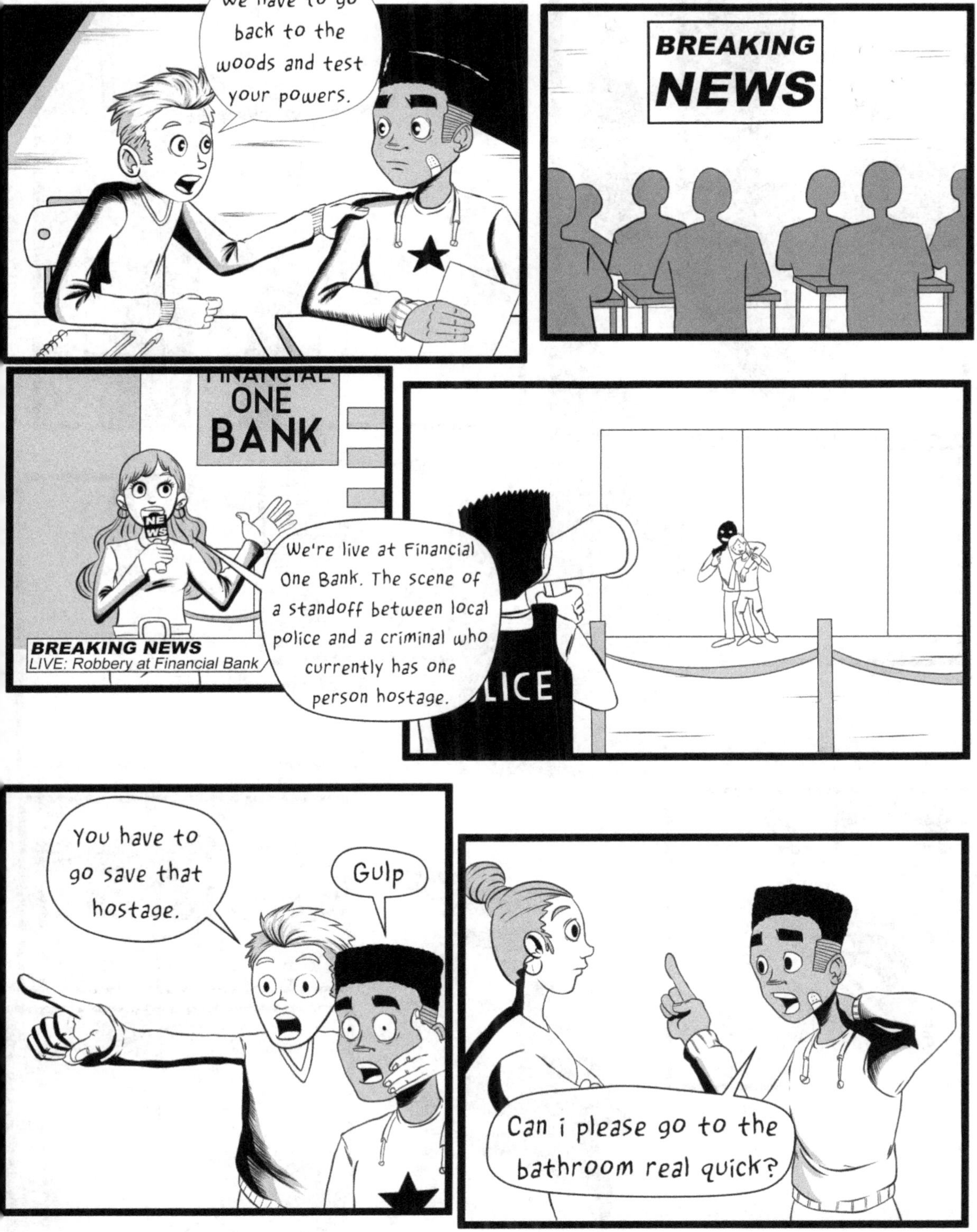

We have to go back to the woods and test your powers.
BREAKING NEWS
FINANCIAL ONE BANK
NEWS
BREAKING NEWS
LIVE: Robbery at Financial Bank
We're live at Financial One Bank. The scene of a standoff between local police and a criminal who currently has one person hostage.
LICE
You have to go save that hostage.
Gulp
Can i please go to the bathroom real quick?

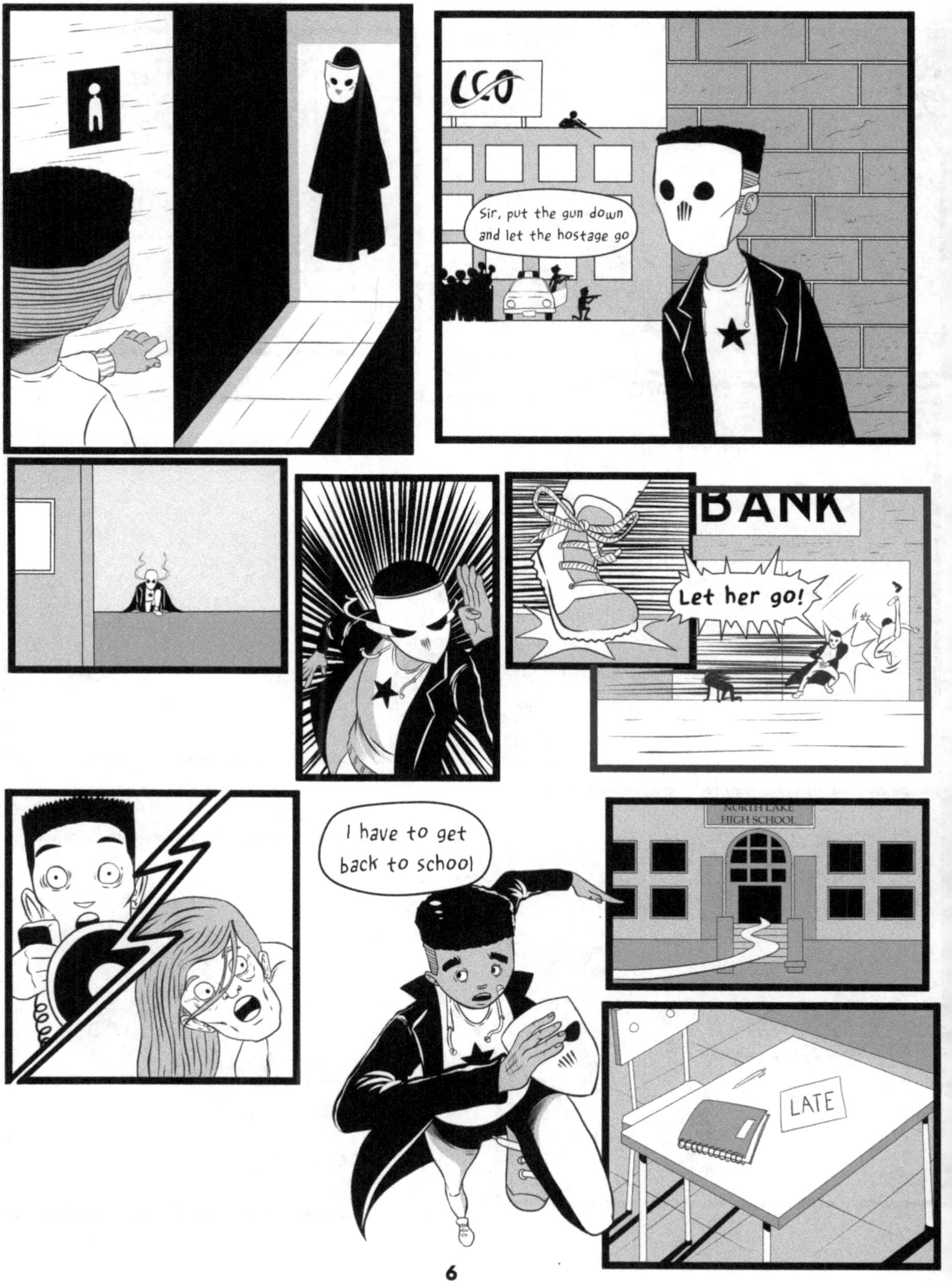

LEO
Sir, put the gun down and let the hostage go
BANK
Let her go!
I have to get back to school
NORTH LAKE HIGH SCHOOL
LATE

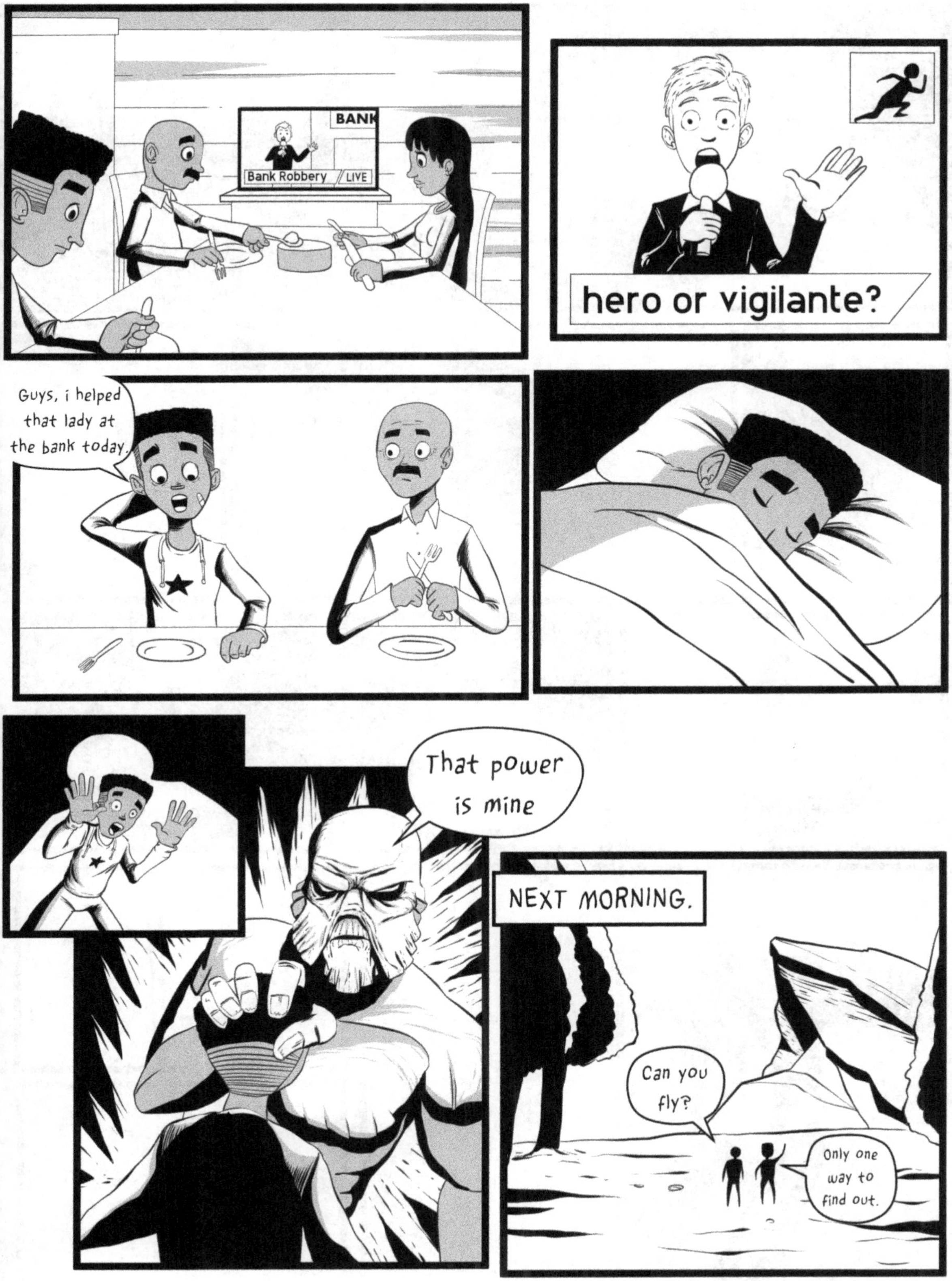
BANK
Bank Robbery
LIVE
hero or vigilante?
Guys, i helped that lady at the bank today.
That power is mine
NEXT MORNING.
Can you fly?
Only one way to find out.

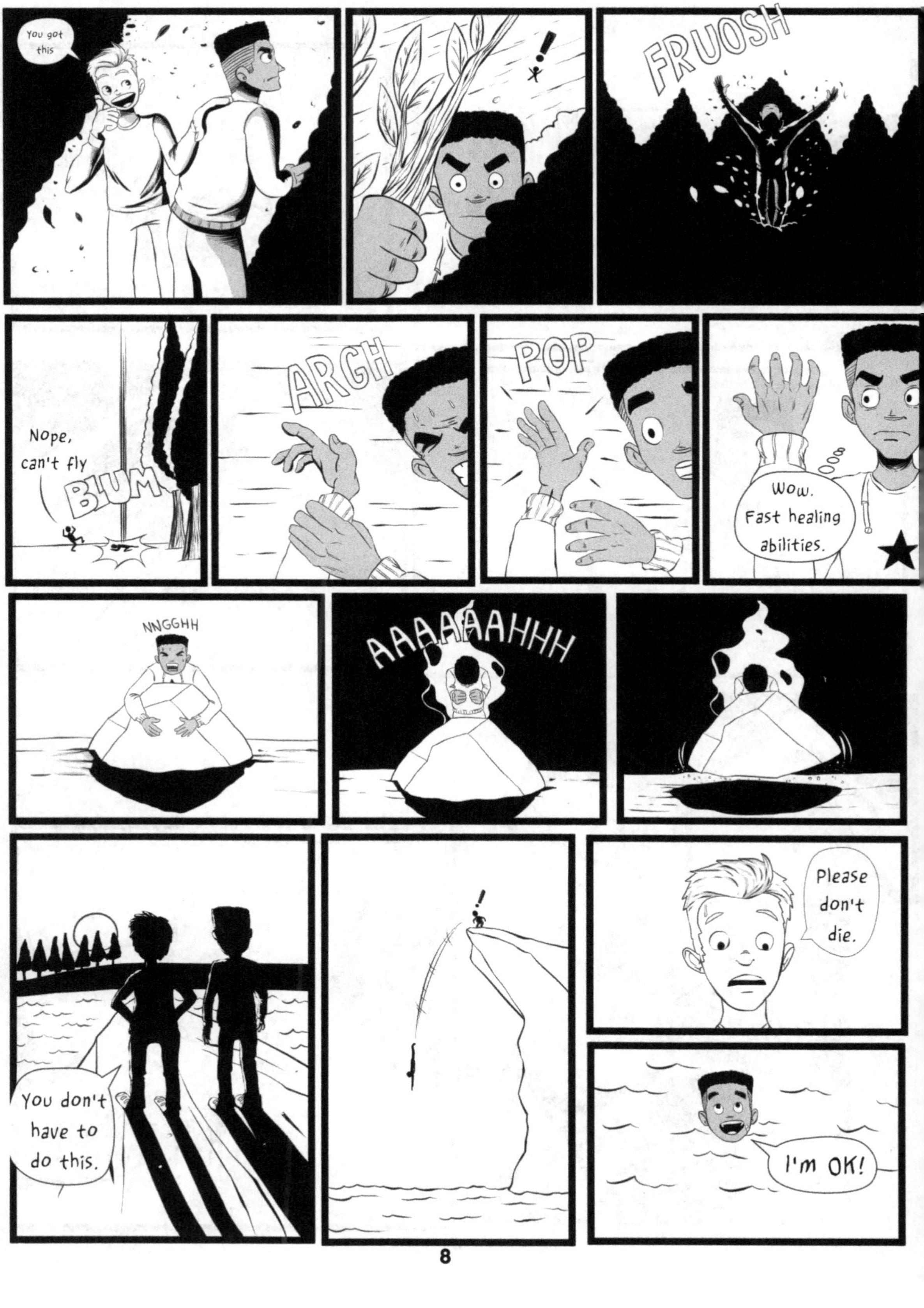
You got this
FRUOSH
Nope, can't fly
BLUM
ARGH
POP
Wow. Fast healing abilities.
NNGGHH
AAAAAAHHH
You don't have to do this.
Please don't die.
I'm OK!

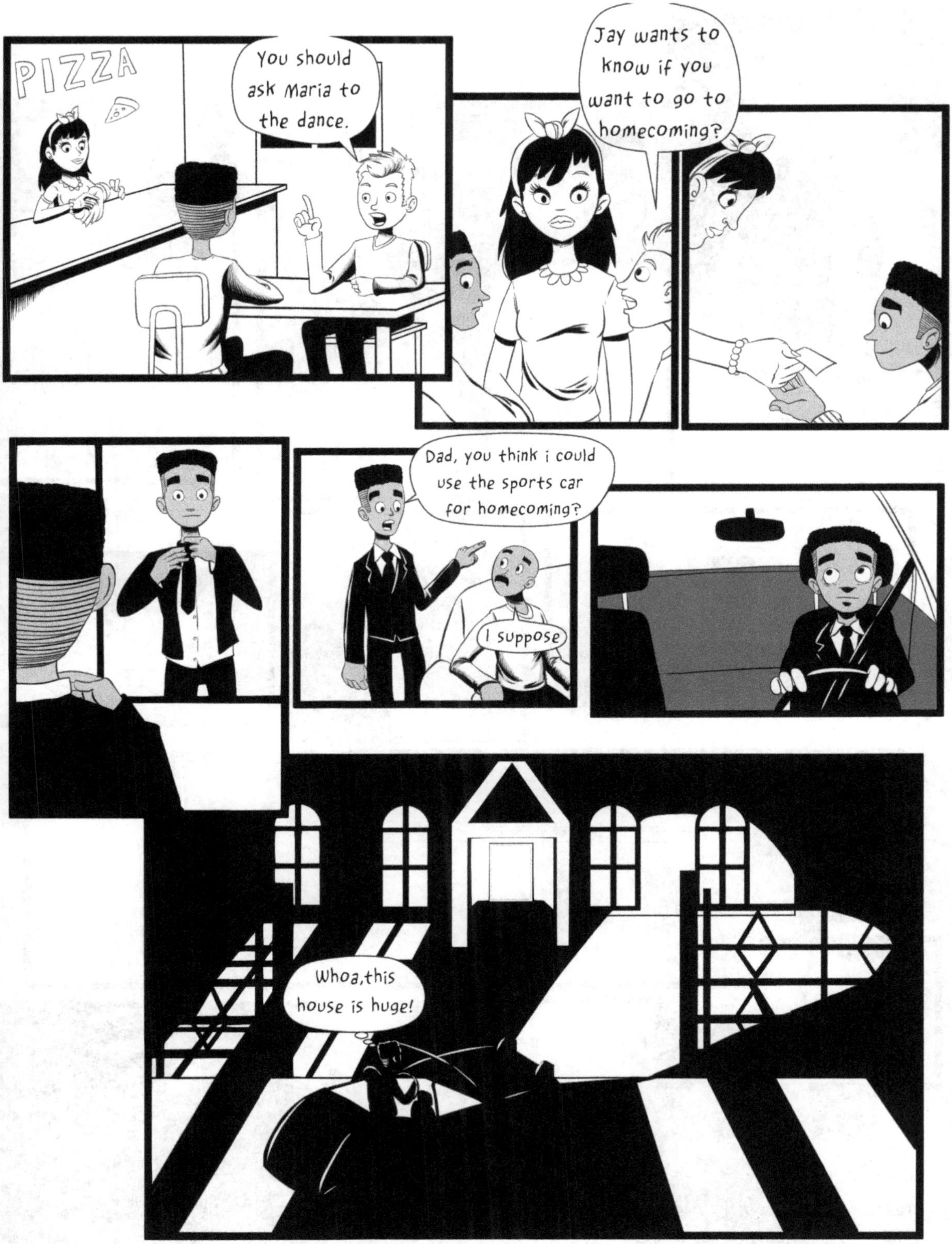
PIZZA
You should ask Maria to the dance.
Jay wants to know if you want to go to homecoming?
Dad, you think i could use the sports car for homecoming?
I suppose
Whoa,this house is huge!

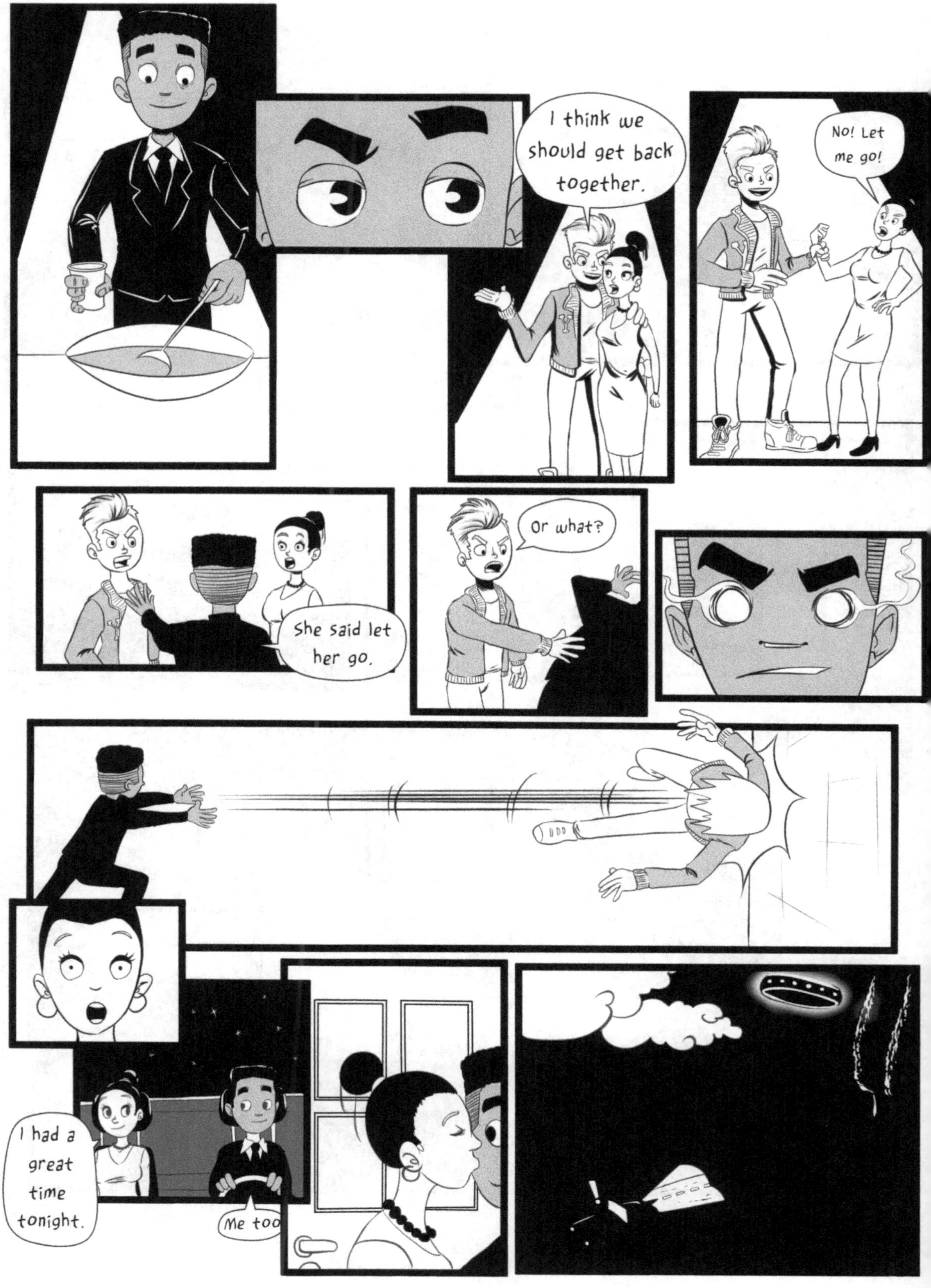
I think we should get back together.
No! Let me go!
She said let her go.
Or what?
I had a great time tonight.
Me too

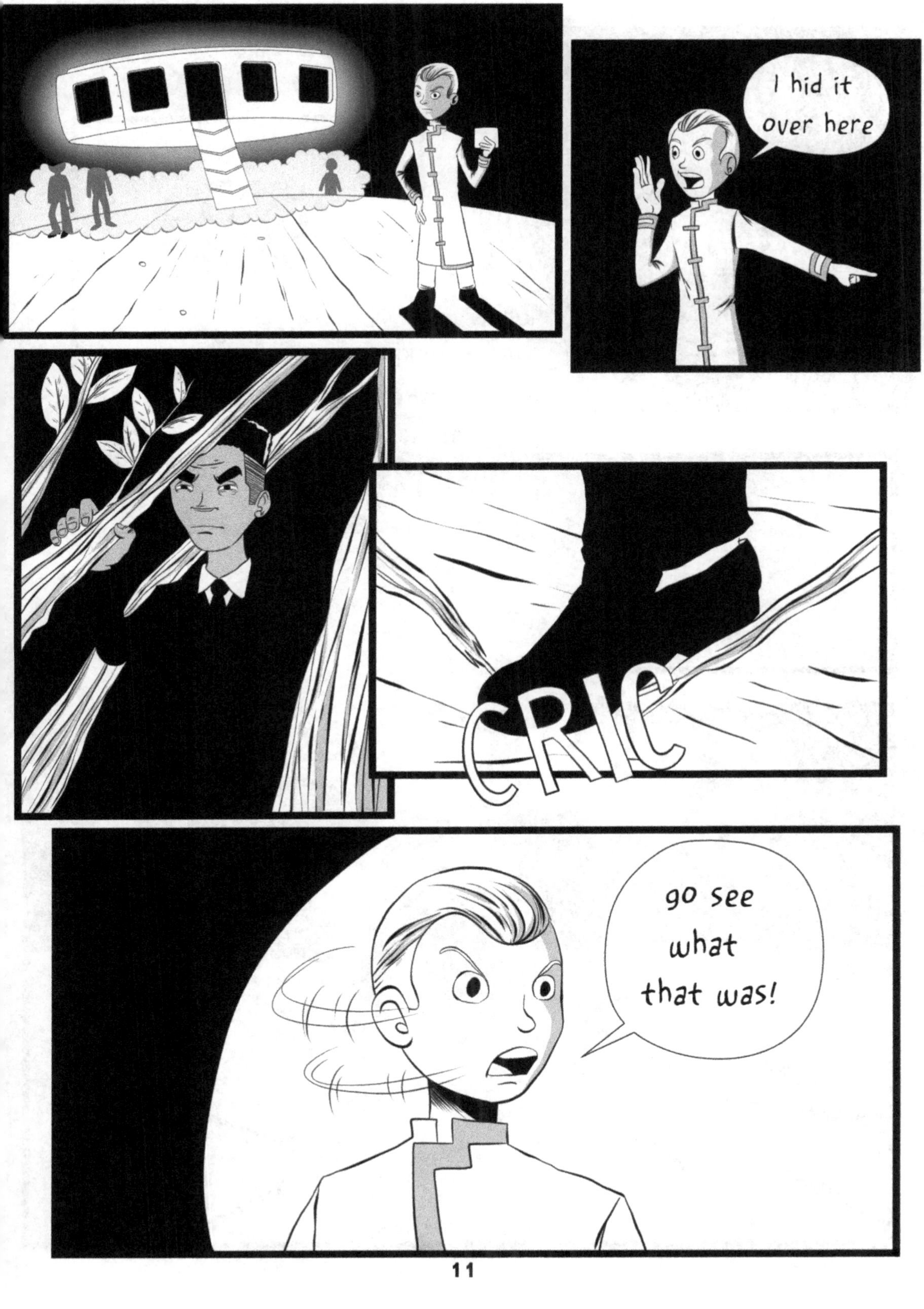
I hid it over here
CRIC
go see what that was!

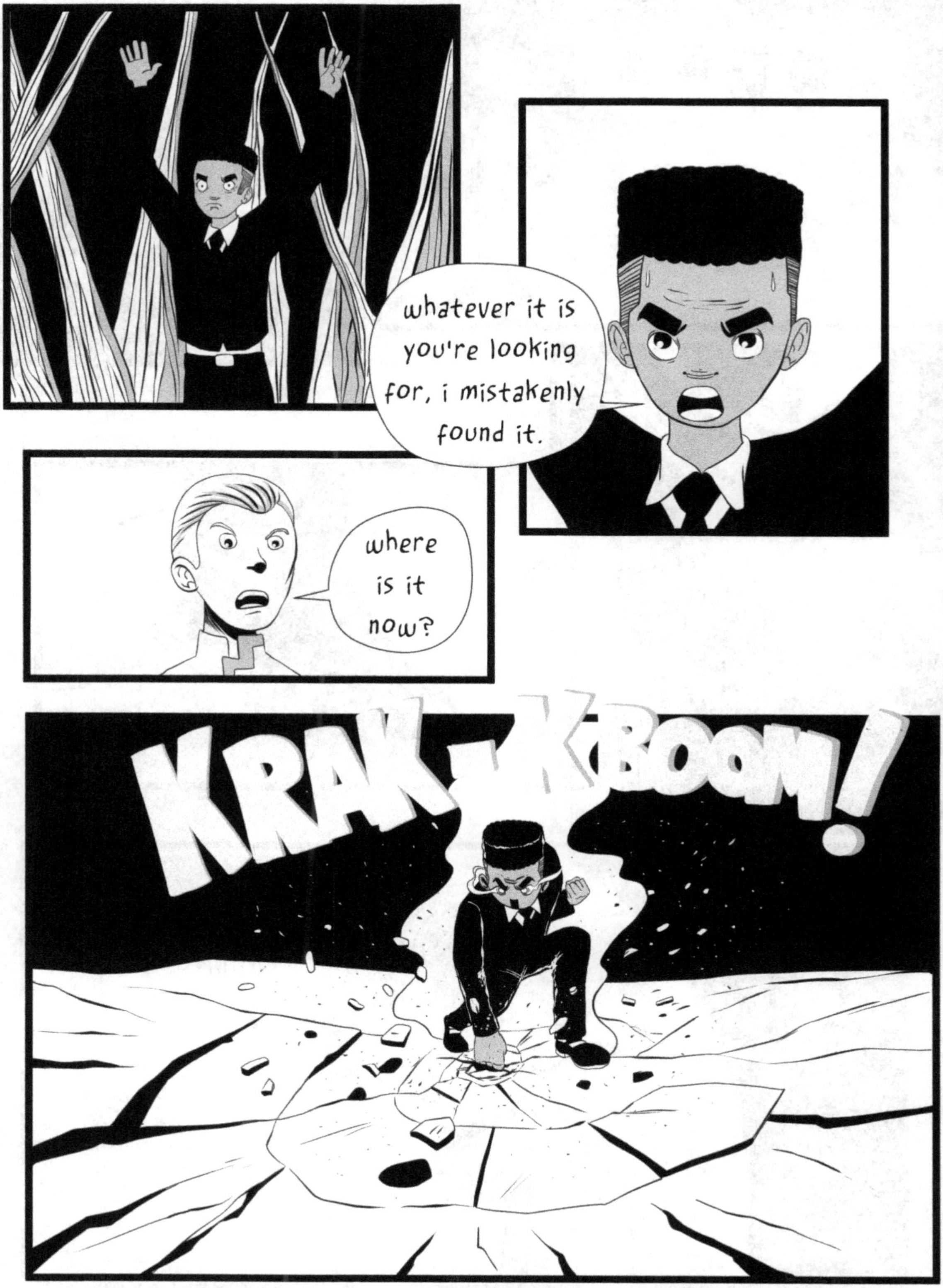
whatever it is you're looking for, i mistakenly found it.
where is it now?
KRAK
KBOOM!

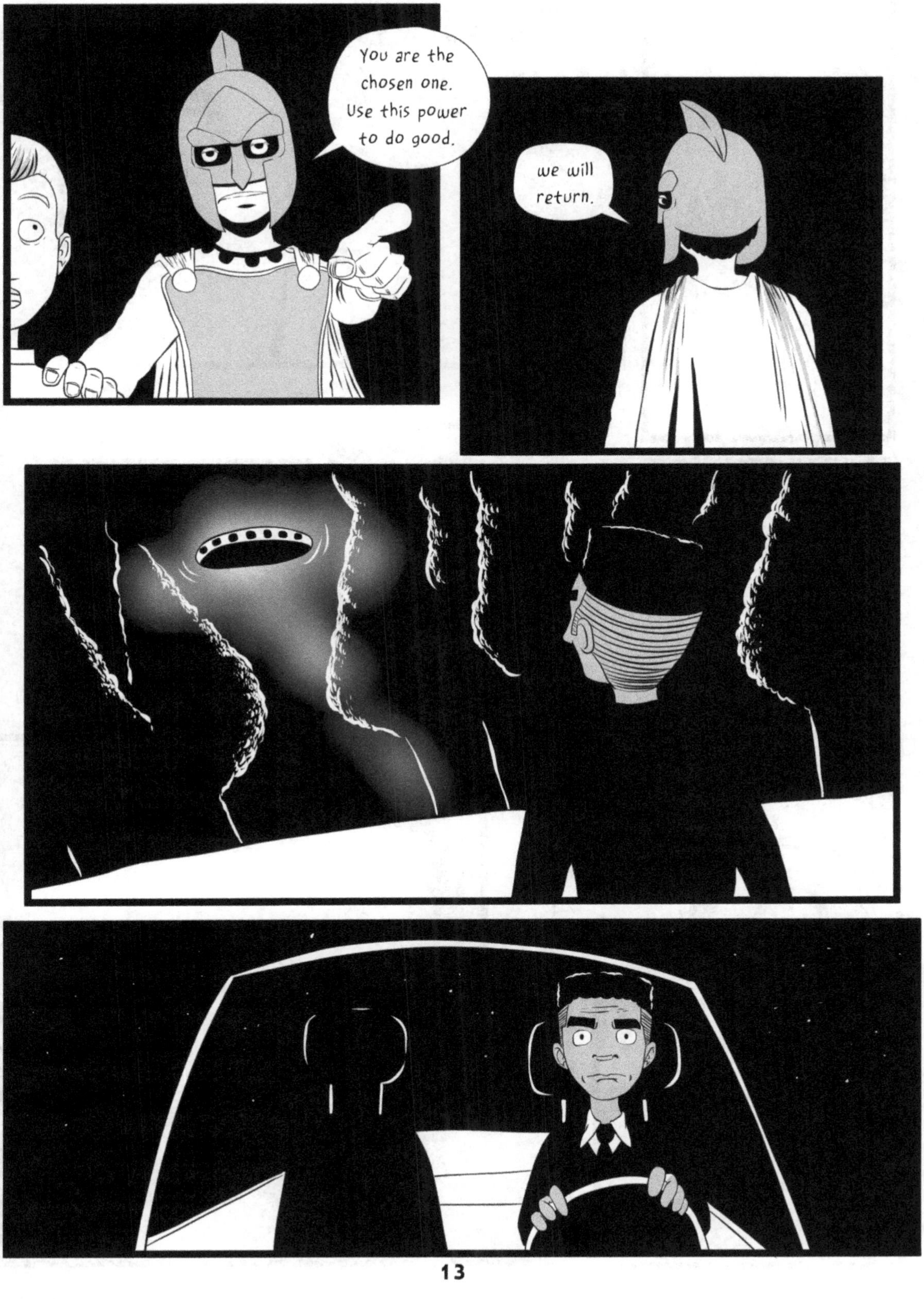
You are the chosen one. Use this power to do good.
we will return.

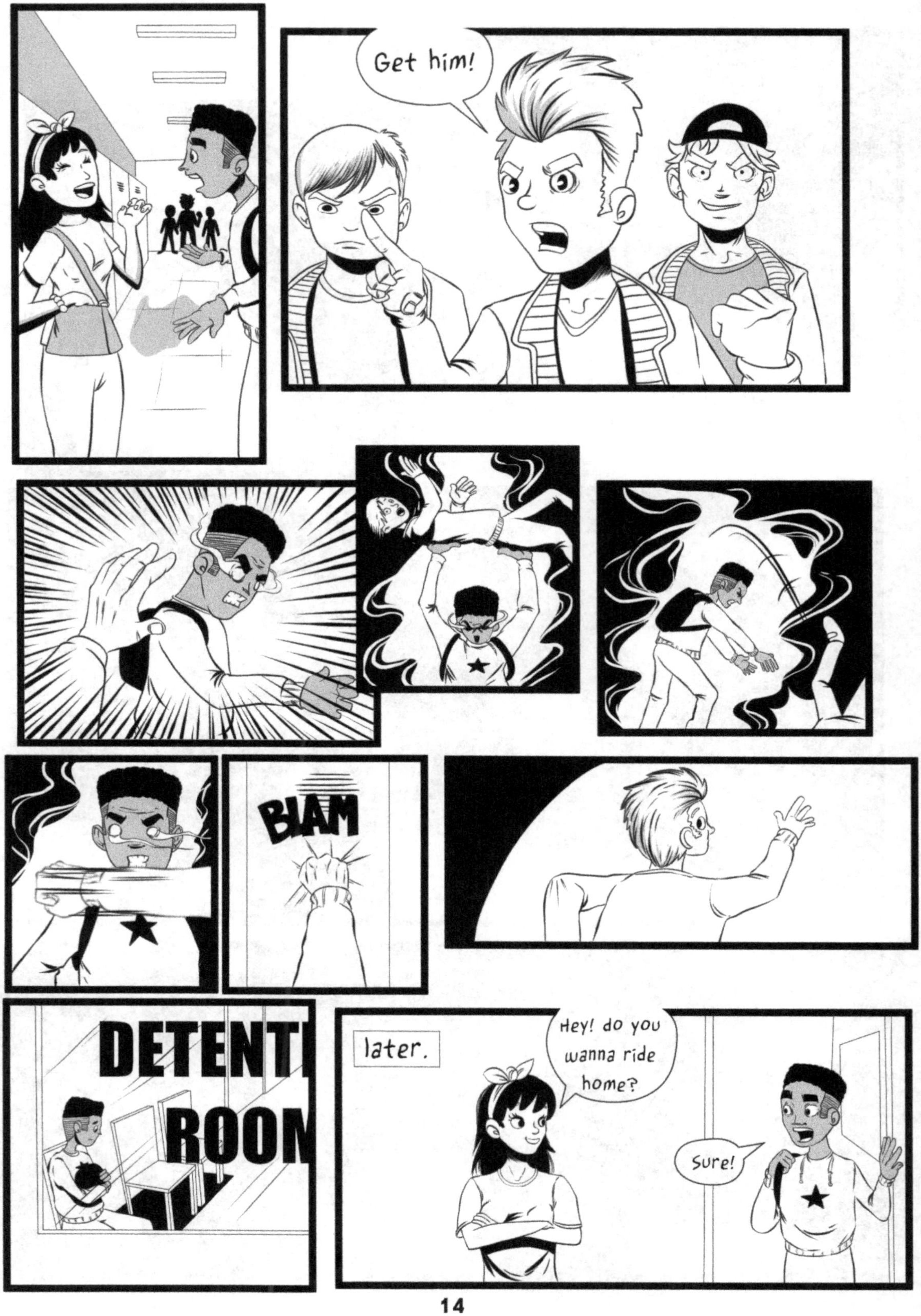
Get him!
BIAM
DETENTI
ROOM
later.
Hey! do you wanna ride home?
Sure!

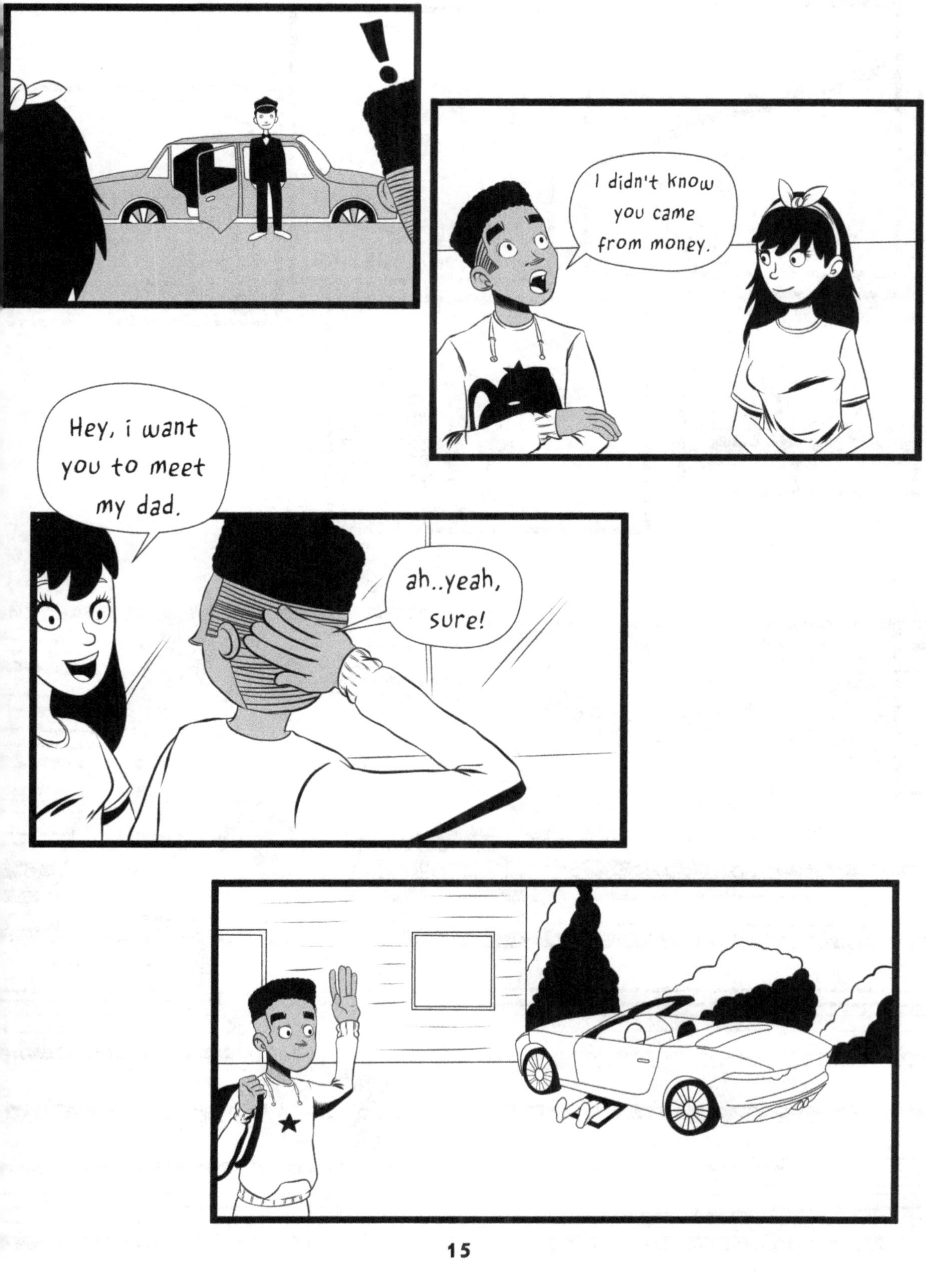
!
I didn't know you came from money.
Hey, i want you to meet my dad.
ah..yeah, sure!

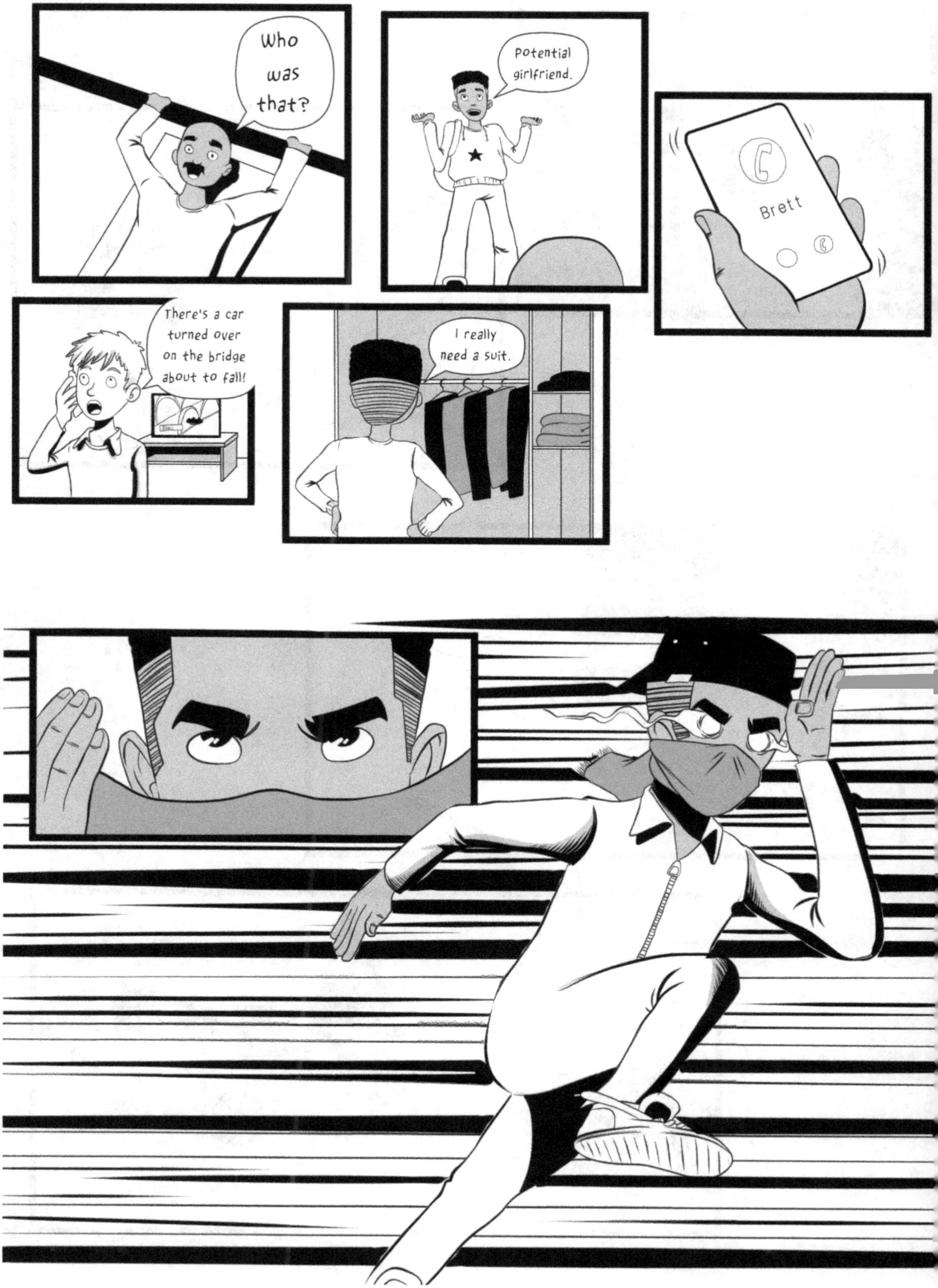
Who was that?
Potential girlfriend.
Brett
There's a car turned over on the bridge about to fall!
I really need a suit.

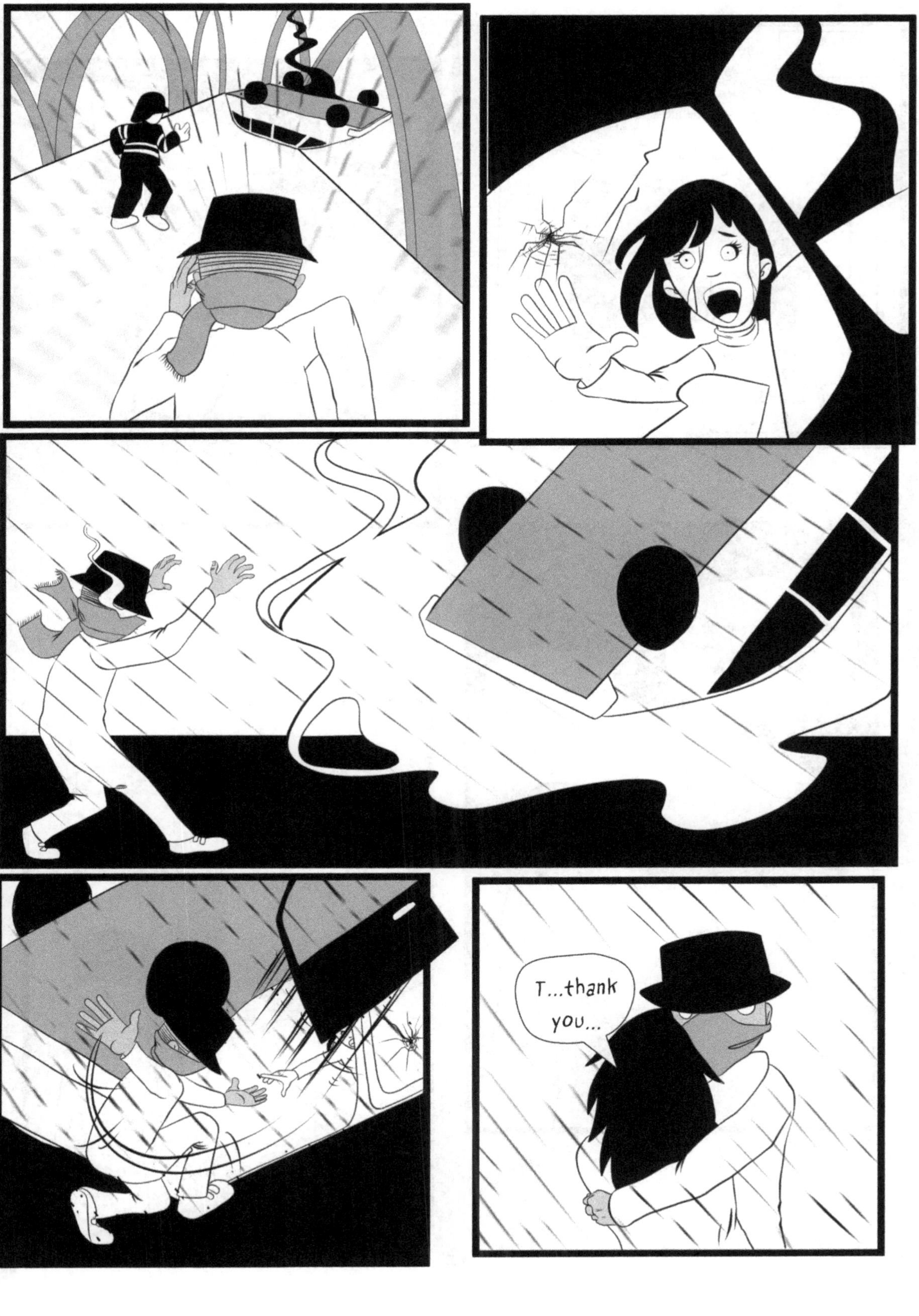
T...thank
you...

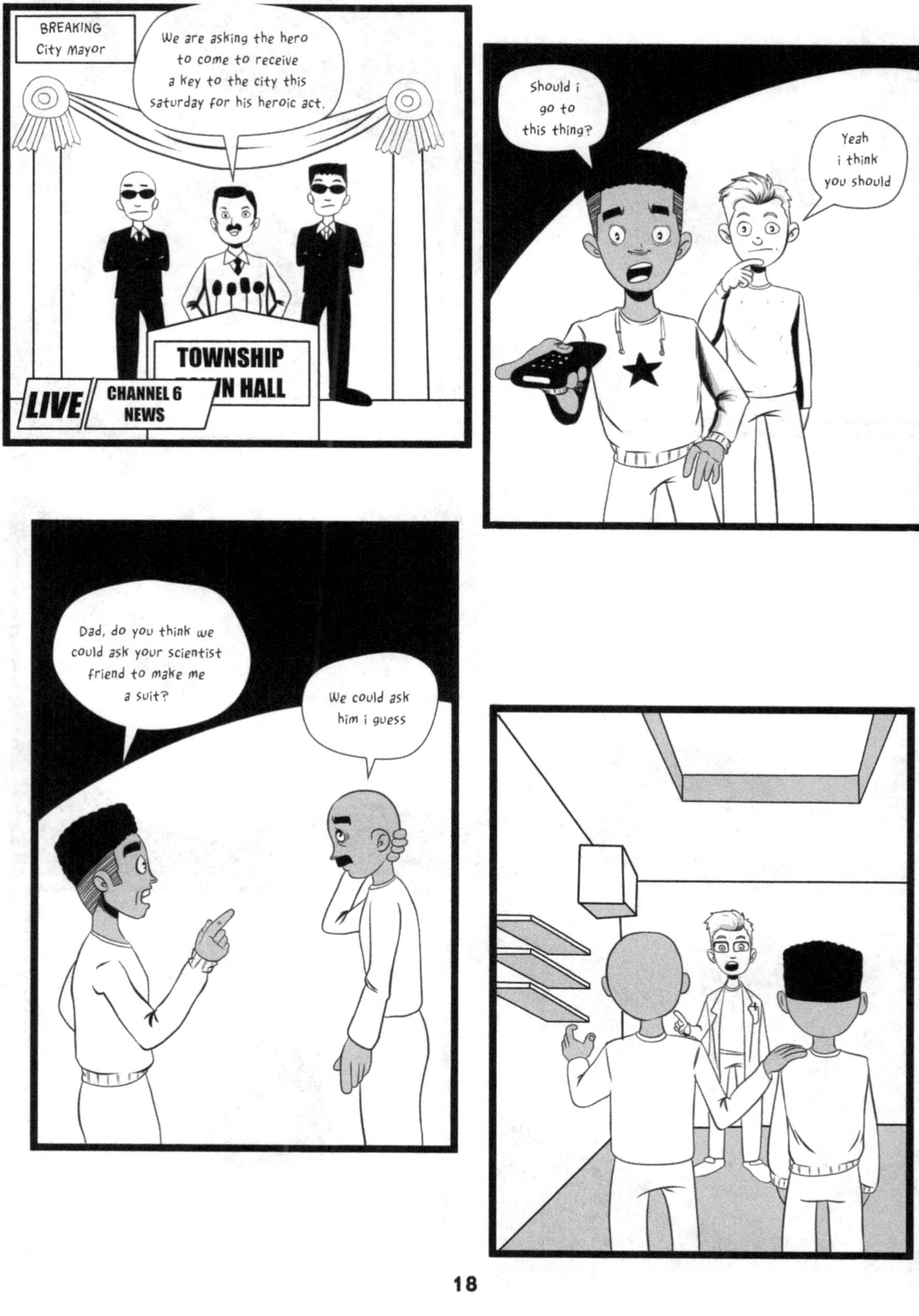
BREAKING
City Mayor
We are asking the hero to come to receive a key to the city this saturday for his heroic act.
TOWNSHIP
IN HALL
LIVE
CHANNEL 6 NEWS
Should i go to this thing?
Yeah i think you should
Dad, do you think we could ask your scientist friend to make me a suit?
We could ask him i guess

Give me a couple of days. I've been working on something for an occasion like this.

A couple of days later at the lab..

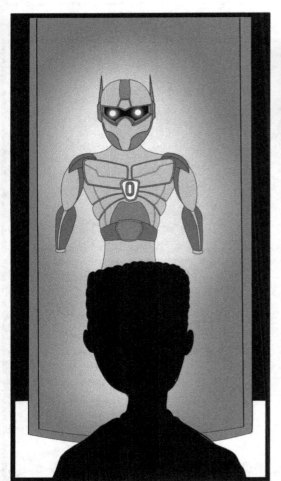

So, here's the suit. What do you think?

We think you need a name!

19

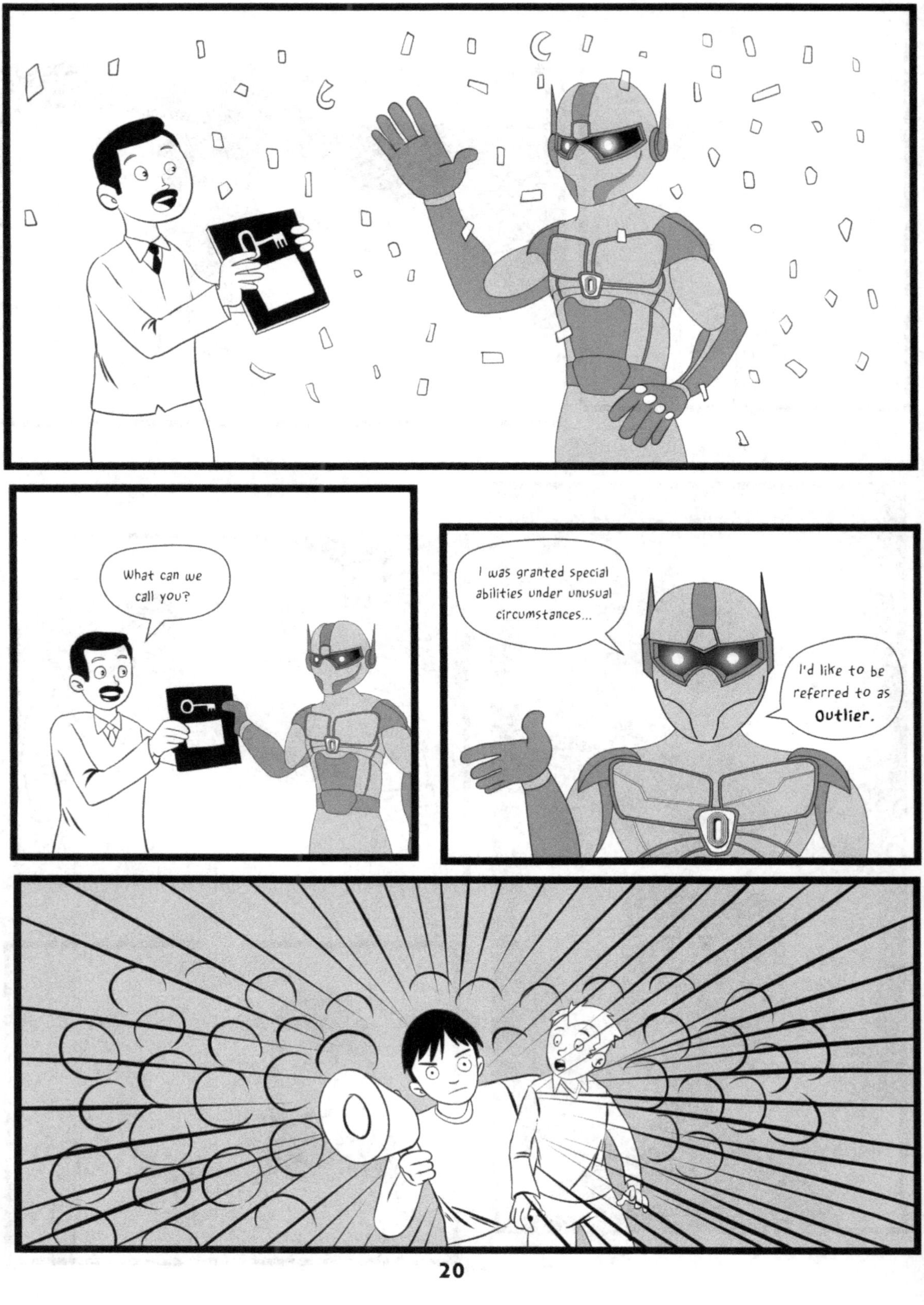
What can we call you?
I was granted special abilities under unusual circumstances...
I'd like to be referred to as **Outlier.**

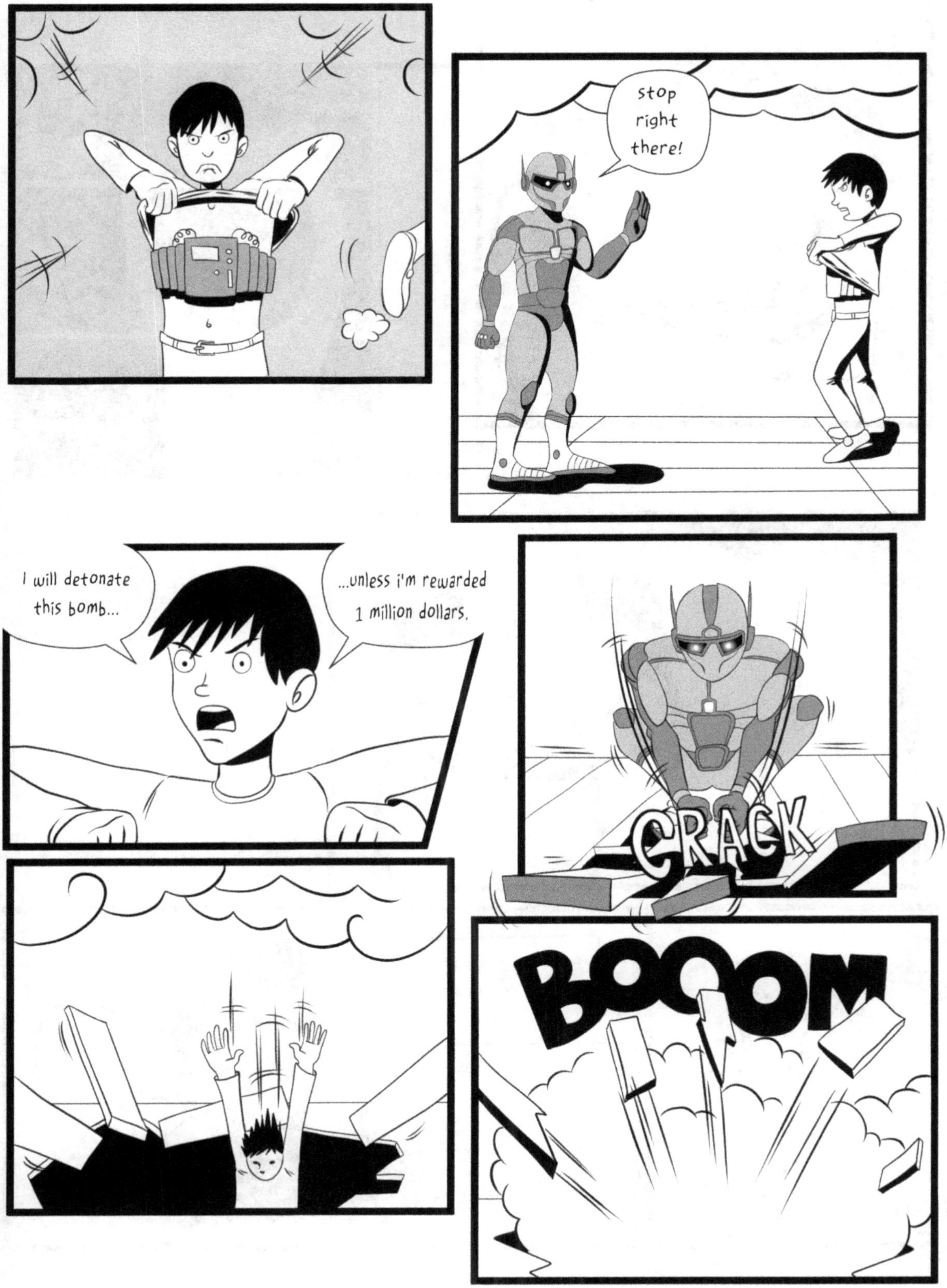
stop right there!
I will detonate this bomb...
...unless i'm rewarded 1 million dollars.
CRACK
BOOOM

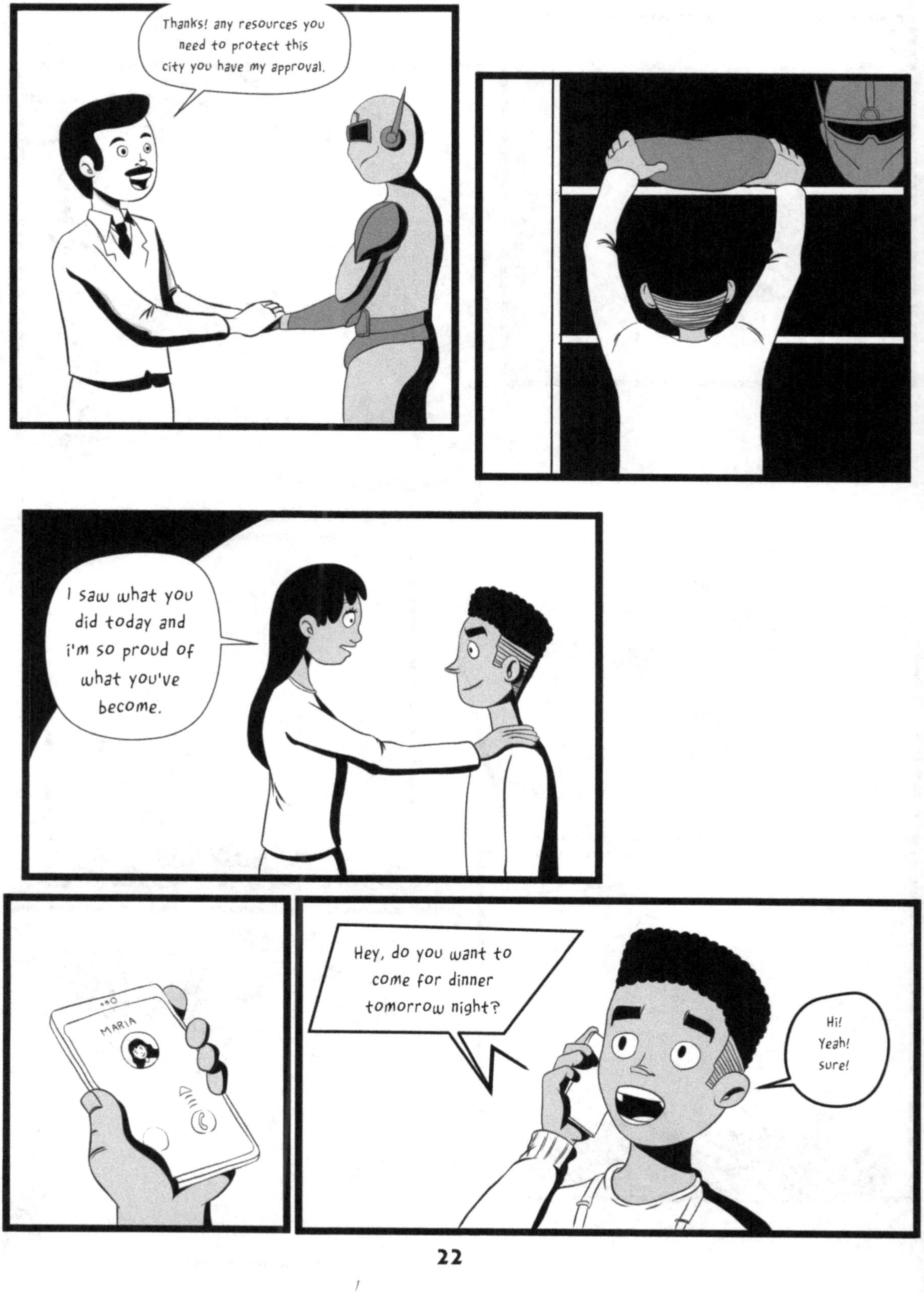

Thanks! any resources you need to protect this city you have my approval.
I saw what you did today and i'm so proud of what you've become.
MARIA
Hey, do you want to come for dinner tomorrow night?
Hi! Yeah! sure!

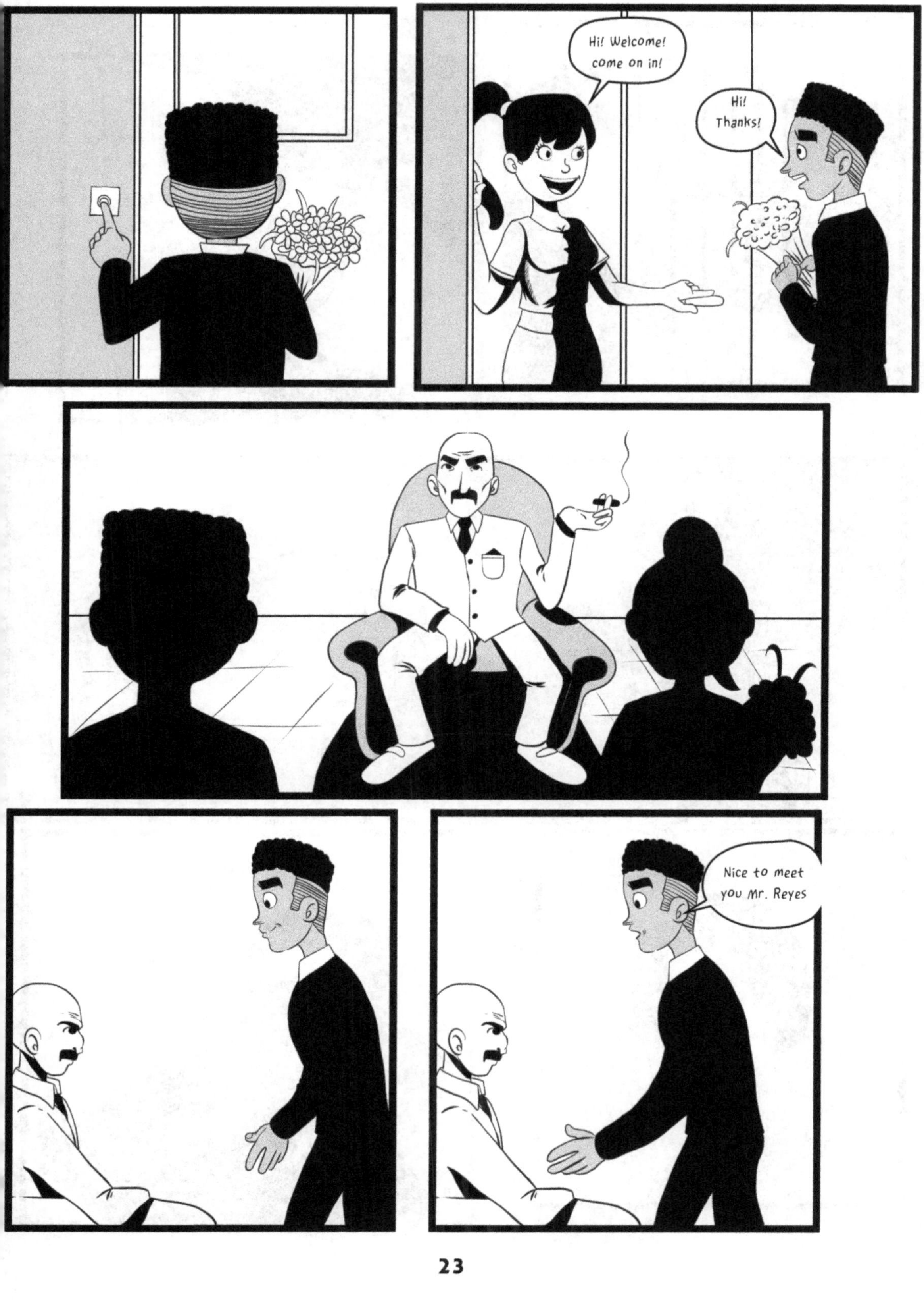
Hi! Welcome!
come on in!
Hi!
Thanks!
Nice to meet
you Mr. Reyes

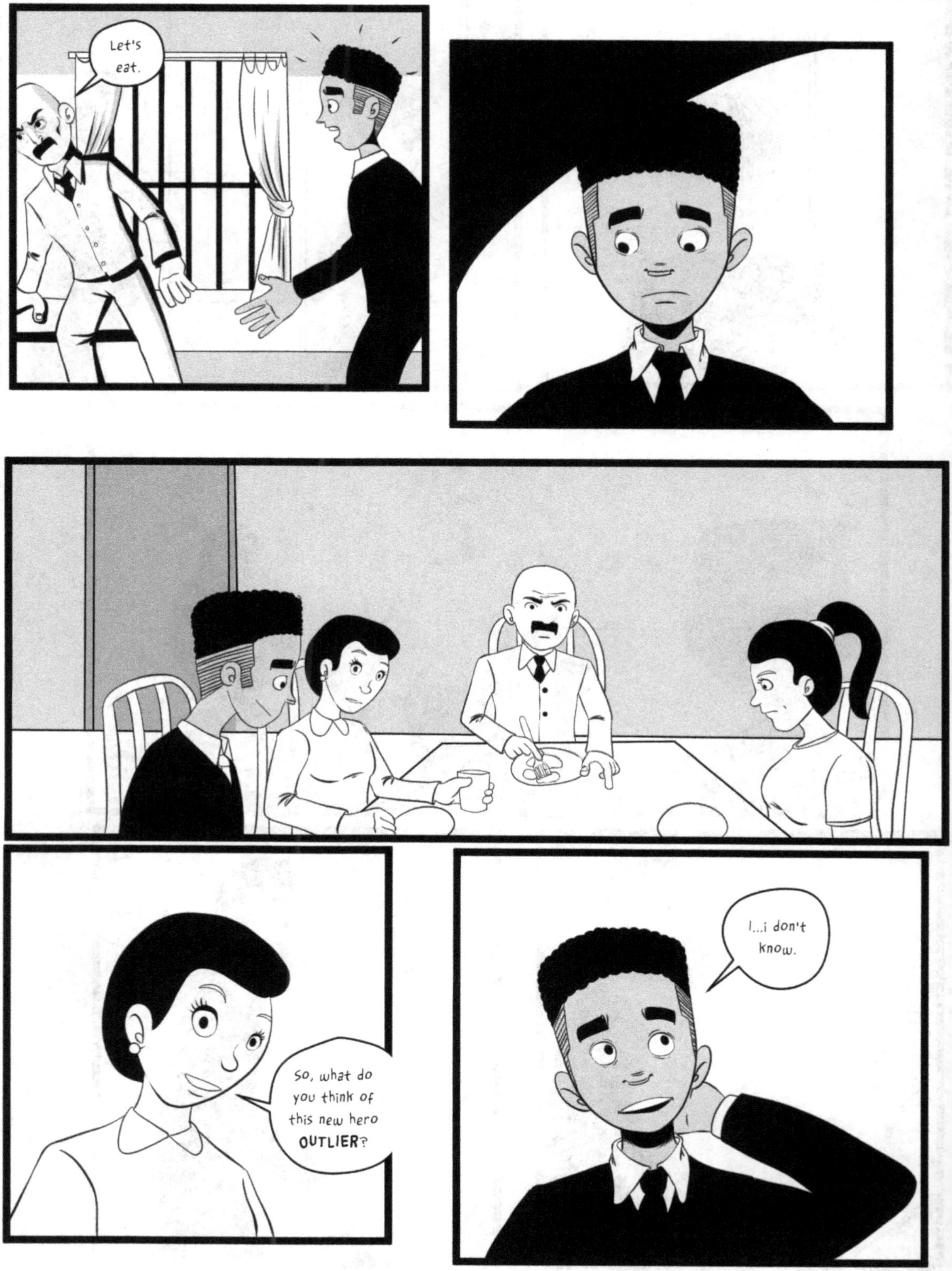
Let's eat.
So, what do you think of this new hero OUTLIER?
I...i don't know.

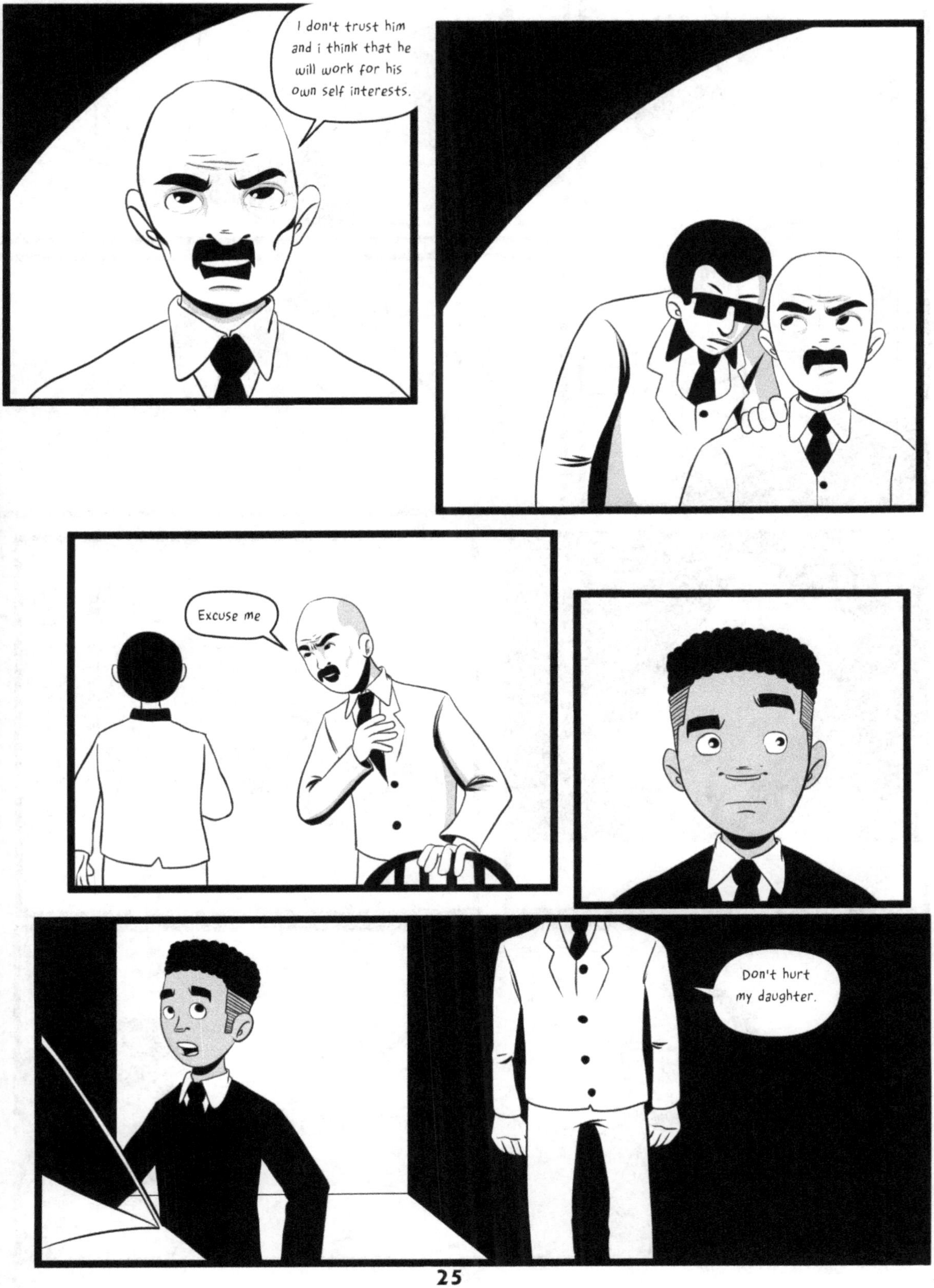
I don't trust him and i think that he will work for his own self interests.
Excuse me
Don't hurt my daughter.

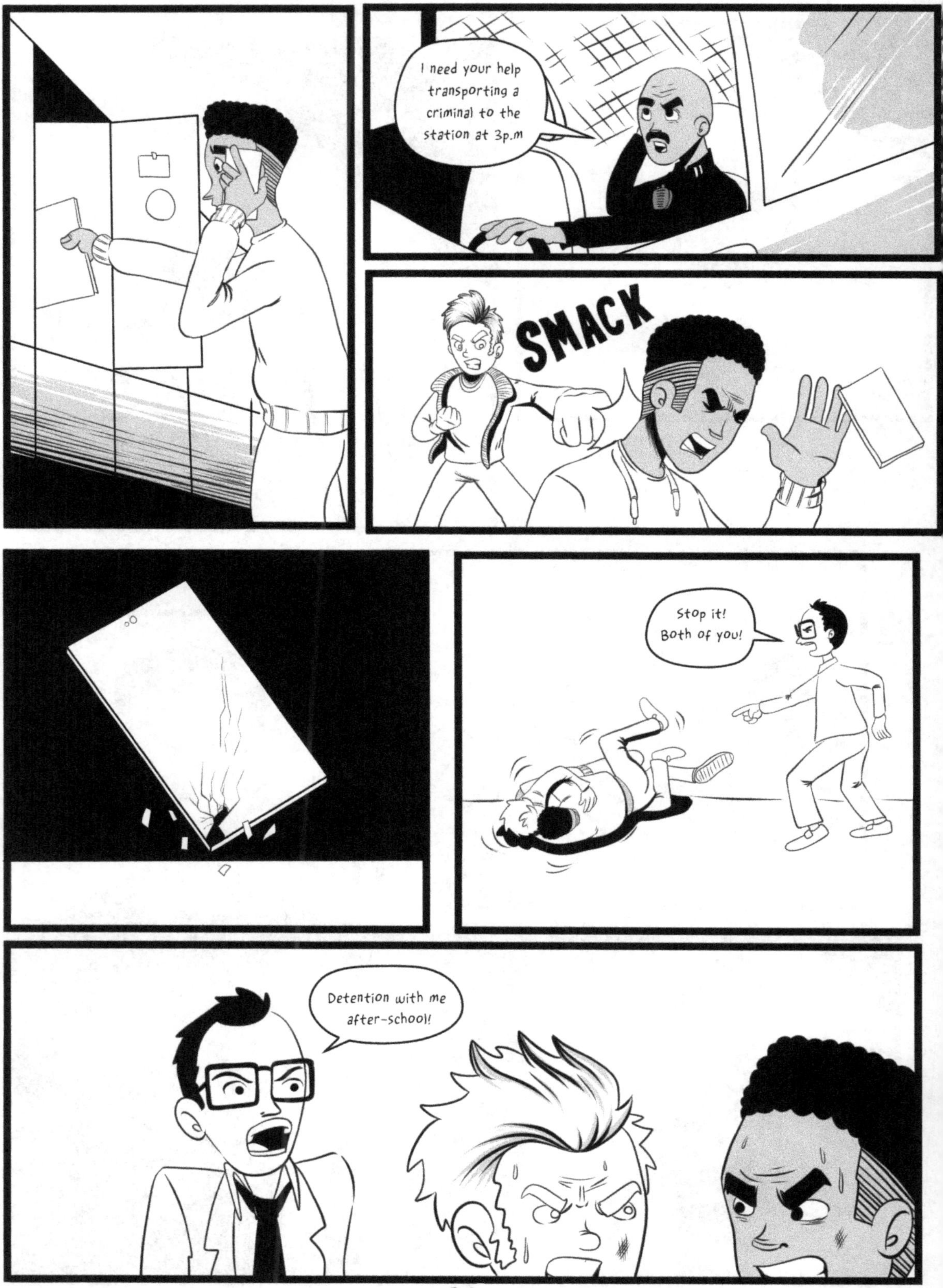

I need your help transporting a criminal to the station at 3p.m
SMACK
Stop it! Both of you!
Detention with me after-school!

CPSIA information can be obtained
at www.ICGtesting.com
Printed in the USA
JSHW030741280921
19079JS00003B/8

9 781662 917257